How Not Loving Taught Me To Love

Dhruvi Shah Mota

Presentation by *BookLeaf Publishing*

Web: www.bookleafpub.com

E-mail: info@bookleafpub.com

ISBN: 9789357741880

First edition 2023

I dedicate this book to my only and forever love, Pratiik Mota.

To dad, mom, Himani & Mirang for traversing the pursuit of love with me.

To mummy, papa, Parshav & Khushboo for loving me from afar.

To Shruti, Aneri, Ruchika, Ruchi, Arzoo, Yesha and countless other friends who have patiently been waiting and encouraging me to write my "book".

To Sonali miss, thank you for being my biggest cheerleader.

ACKNOWLEDGEMENT

None of who I am is possible without the people who make me.

I have to acknowledge how much of a role my husband plays in my creative pursuits, being non-judgemental and ever-encouraging.

My immediate family supports me through all my moods. This includes my father, mother, sister, and brother-in-law.

I never knew that getting married and having a second family could be as supportive as my own. My mother-in-law, father-in-law, brother-in-law, and co-sister have been my pillars of support in tough times.

And finally, there are some sisters and girlfriends and friends who have been egging me on to write a book since time immemorial. This is for them.

I learnt to write and was appreciated for it, by my school teacher, who I grew with. She is my inspiration!

PREFACE

I loved love. In my art books, my notebooks, and my journals, I tried different iterations of the word, love. I'm a sucker for anything heart-shaped. When I first connected with my husband, I used to listen to his heartbeat to feel calm. LOVE. It is an emotion, an expression, a reason for being and not feeling the best. Love makes the world go round but could want you to not exist at all. LOVE...

Many before me have explored this subject, and I have my words to add to this. I sincerely hope that in the journey of this book of poetry, you feel the emotion and also want to spread it with joy. Enjoy reading!

The Rush

Tumbling out incoherently,
Like a floodgate had been opened,
I remember my heart beating fast,
That feeling of "butterflies fluttering",
When someone suggested 'he' had a 'crush' on
me.

I was too young to make meaning of it,
We were too young to understand it.

The extent of our relationship was,
Saying "I miss you" and "I like you,"
Holding hands in an empty classroom.

Alas, this "relationship" lasted,
All of some months,
When he ended it,
Because he liked another girl,
Albeit from my class.

Puppy love was the term,
As I would come to understand it,
Years later.

This taught me,
I could have emotions that I didn't comprehend.

The Bittersweet

Adolescence is a tricky time,
Your parents try to teach you what's right,
And everyone around wants to try the wrong.

I wouldn't say wrong,
But I did "fall for someone".

Only because pop culture taught me so,
I believed my best friend,
Who was one of the most popular boys,
Would love me,
And I would love back.

It was tricky navigating this relationship,
We were inseparable,
Yet very aware of how separate we were.

As you might have predicted,
This was a story,
Of my best friend falling for the popular girl,
And me being the listening ear.

This pattern continued into our adult life,
Until I couldn't take it anymore.

We exchange texts on our birthdays,
Twice a year.

3

And that's the extent of this
"Childhood best friendship".

Luckily, as an adult, I now know,
What a 'best friend' truly is.

This taught me,
It's not important to label relationships.

The Important One

Whether Freud was right,
I'm not sure.

But at the end of every day,
When I got back from school,
I tidied up before Dad came home.

He had this persona,
That could be considered strict.

He would give me advice,
With the expectation,
that it would be implemented.

Living up to the promises,
I made to him,
Was extremely important to me.

Being back home,
At a curfew time he suggested,
Was something I feared if not followed.

But he showed me the world,
He showed me his world.

He protected me, cajoled me,
Brought a smile to my face,
Showed up every single time,
I needed him.

He would continue to be,
Better, more open, more understanding,
Than I knew then.

But this taught me,
My dad was the male figure,
That would shape my interactions with men.

The In-Between

School and college are fine,
Because every relationship,
Forged in these institutions,
Mostly comes with an expiry date.

So did mine.
I didn't have 'relationships'.
I just dated,
Until it became difficult to,
And then called it off.

Some of it was filled with
Gushing emotions.
Some of it was filled with,
The first traces of anxiety.
Some of it,
Really didn't matter,
In the long run.

But it was something.
Awkward yet sweet.
Painful yet necessary.

This taught me,
"Growing up" was a phase.

The "First Real Love"

For the longest time,
After it was over,
I believed it to be,
"The first real love".

It had all the makings of it.

A recognition among friends,
And his parents.

Those mandatory celebrations,
Of important days and dates.

Those "fights" and the need to "make up".

The learnings as an adult,
The influence on choices and decisions.

The pride of the "label".

We were everything to each other,
Only not open about it.

At this age,
It would be complicated.

It was either marriage,
Or a no-go.

Unfortunately,
We didn't have the gumption,
To carry it forward,
into the real world.

So, it was a no-go.

This taught me,
Just how painful losing love can be.

The "Arranged Date"

Let's consider this number one.
In the many arranged dates to come.

Set up by a matchmaker,
Egged on by my parents,
Was this meeting with a "stranger".

Who would go on to smoke,
While I looked in the other direction.
Who would ask really personal questions,
Only to make a judgement of me.
Who would make inappropriate jokes,
Which let slip he was an anti-feminist.

He would then spread the word,
That I drink wine,
And of course, that would make me,
"That kind of a woman,"
in our tightly knit community.

It was a failure,
A forerunner for the years to come.

This taught me,
There is a very closed "market" for marriages.

The One That Was Almost Done

Sitting at my favourite restaurant,
Waiting for him to come.

As one usually would,
For these "dates".

He was quite smooth,
Said all the right things,
Was the optimum amount of "cool".

We met again,
This time, at a Starbucks.
And he asked me to wait,
At a table, while he brought,
Our "order".

A few minutes later,
A waiter with a plate of,
"Java Chip Cookies",
Was looking for the right recipient.

Turned out, they were for me,
Sent by my "husband",
Because I used the word "sweet",
In all our texting.

It was at the fourth date,
He professed he was ready to,
Marry me. The ultimate goal, apparently.

When I innocently blurted,
I wasn't 'attracted' to him.

That was the last I saw of him.

And he crushed the hopes of the
Matchmaker too.

This taught me,
Be transparent, even when egos are fragile.

The Process

By the fifth or sixth,
"Arranged date",
One has a process.

I knew, because I had checked,
With my single friends,
In the same melting pot of emotions.

You wear certain colours,
Certain kinds of clothes,
Pick a "medium" range restaurant,
Show up in a "certain" car,
Say all the "appropriate things",
Make merry,
Go home, and wait for a response.

Sorry, your daughter is too short,
For our son,
Sorry, our son doesn't think,
She's the right fit.
Sorry, our son is still making his way,
In the world, and your daughter,
Doesn't seem to fit the bill.
Sorry, your daughter is on the "healthier" side,
and won't look good with our son.

Sorry, your daughter (fill in the blank).
Sorry, our son (fill in the blank).
13

This taught me,
There were too many blanks to fill.

The Apps

Kicking tradition in the belly,
I was heroic enough to get on,
The Apps. Yes, Tinder, Hinge, Aisle, Bumble,
and so on.

Every app was different.
Everyone had a different goal.
A sea of humans,
Floating on these apps,
Having multiple conversations,
Two truths and a lie,
Sometimes catfishing, or baring it all.

Nobody remembered how they got on,
Yet nobody wanted to go anywhere.
It was just a wham and a bam,
That most were looking for.

It got exhausting, the swiping,
The persona, the upkeep, the... everything.

So, one would get off the apps,
Try their luck the old-fashioned way,
Get back on the apps,
Ready with a fresh approach.

Guilty as charged,
I was a contender.

This taught me,
There was nothing I wouldn't try.

The Support System

Meet mom.
She was in her early fifties,
When these shenanigans
Were taking place.

She had one agenda,
To see me happily married.

She didn't have too many conditions,
Or questions even.

She was happy as long as I was.

That was the toughie.
She wished me luck before each date.
Both of us stayed hopeful.

She would 'talk' to the 'moms' of the boys,
She would hear every detail of every date.

'How was it?' She would ask at the door.

I was disappointed to disappoint her.

But not once did she flinch.
She had an unwavering faith.
When no one else did.

She was my mom. She would get me married.
Most days, it was this belief
That carried me forward too.

This taught me,
The woman who birthed me,
Played the most important role in my life.

The Dejection

Tried it all.
Been through it all.
Set myself up for failure.

Groaned. Given up.

Does love even exist?
I would ask myself.

All I wanted was a ray of hope.
For myself.

In front of me
Were loveless marriages.
Were adjustments and compromises.
Were giving in and then giving up.

I had 'flaws' apparently.
I was fat. I was forward.
I was too far out there.
I wasn't mingling enough.
Everything was confusing.
Yet it made sense for some.

Every time a friend of mine got hitched.
It served a reminder that I wasn't.

The clock was ticking.
When I decided to put a stop to it all.

And do this my way. With love.

What that meant was yet to be explained.
But I knew. I knew if I did it with love.
Love would reciprocate.

This taught me,
The only person one should rely on is
themselves.

The Beginning Of Love

As you know by now,
I had done it all.
And hadn't borne the fruit of the effort.

It was at this time in my life,
I came across 'self-love', "law of attraction",
'manifestation'.

I didn't question it.
I just put all my faith in this new practice.

I decided to love myself first.
Without knowing how or why.
I just did.

If I wanted to eat at a fancy restaurant,
I went by myself,
Told a perplexed server, "Table for two for one
of me".
And then enjoyed the dinner as though I was on
a date.

If I wanted to watch a play,
I would purchase a ticket,
Sit in the front row,

And watch as though someone was holding my
hand.

If I wanted to be 'cuddled',
I would empty the side of the bed,
I wasn't sleeping on,
And imagine the pillow I was hugging,
To be my significant other.

Even if I wanted to go for a drive,
I would keep the passenger seat empty and
clean,
Turn on music we would 'both' like.

I even had a vision board,
With pictures, and words,
Of the 'ring' from the 'romantic proposal'
Of the 'lehenga' I would wear at our 'winter
wedding'
Of the 'long, happy marriage' I so desired.

You might think I'm crazy,
Or even silly to share this with you.

But I want you to have the learning I did.

This taught me,
Self-love trumps all love.
And some things are worth the wait.

The Entourage

Loosely translated,
These are the people,
Who eventually make
Your wedding party.

I'll start with my little sister,
She tried in every way possible,
To match me, encourage me,
Make me feel heard,
Explain the other's perspective to me.
She stood by me like a rock.

At the time, my sister's boyfriend,
Now her husband, and my brother-in-law,
Who I would leave details of the date with.
Who would amuse me by making fun of my
dates.
Who was there whenever I called.

My sisters from different misters,
My 3 best friends, who painstakingly,
Counselled me, showed up in every way
possible,
Who heard and read updates from all the dates,
Be it phone calls or WhatsApp group chats.

My cousin sister, who was fighting her own love
battle,
Who traversed part of the process with me,
Met me when the "arranged date" was a
no-show,
Hung out with me just because I wanted
company,
Looked over me like an older sister would.

My cousin's wife, my sister-in-law,
Who never felt like an outsider,
In fact, she gave me sound advice,
Heard about every possible 'prospect',
Sometimes even met them to vet them.

Many miscellaneous friends,
Who I can not point out or group,
But were part of the journey in one way or
another.

This taught me,
I had garnered an army around me,
Who loved me unconditionally.

The 'One'

That moment, filled with joy, relief, love, and
nervousness,
When I knew he was 'the one'.
Going back to that moment in that day,
Is like being afloat on a cloud.

We'll have to rewind a little bit.
Not too much.
Just 7 days. From this moment.

I wear glasses. Prescription glasses.
I have, what is called, a cylindrical power.
At this time, I was following,
"The hot belly diet",
And my eye power changed,
To a point I couldn't see anything,
With or without glasses.

I made an appointment with the eye doctor.
He dilated my pupils, as is standard practice.

Visually impaired, I logged on to Hinge,
Started chatting with my now husband.

At the time, neither one of us could have predicted,
What destiny had in store for us.
But we matched, we spoke, we met.
All the while, I had blurry vision.

He was and still is,
A rock solid guy.
I say that, having been married to him,
For more than four years.

He expressed his emotions with honesty,
And I couldn't believe my luck.

We met every day,
In the latter half of September 2017,
Where he felt an irresistible need,
To brave one of Bombay's heaviest rains,
Causing floods all over the city,
Just to come and meet me,
And not break our meeting streak.

It was some nights later,
I would threaten him to confess his feelings for me.
And he did,
And the next morning, when I was leaving his place,
I knew we would be married.

He did too.
A couple of days later,
I told my mom I had feelings for him.
We invited him over for lunch.
Mom approved. Dad gauged.
I celebrated. My search was finally over.

But what was it about him,
That things happened so quickly,
After so many years of the 'search'.

He was honest, he was firm, and he
Loved me enough, and accepted me,
For who I was, in that moment.

This taught me,
Everything has a reason,
You just need to see it.

Our 'Love' Story

A boy from Bhopal.
A girl from Bombay.
Both Kutchi Jain.
Both of marriageable age.
Both in the media.
Both chasing their dreams.

Pratiik and I had so much in common.
That everything else paled.

We wanted to marry each other.
That much was clear.
But we also wanted to do it,
With everyone's agreement and pleasure.

Pratiik and I decided we would marry each
other,
On 21st September 2017.
We finally tied the knot
On 16th December 2018.

A boy from Bhopal.
A girl from Bombay.
Both Kutchi Jain.
Both of marriageable age.

Both in the media.
Both chasing their dreams.

The things that brought us together,
Had the strength to tear us apart.

Before every major event,
Be it our ring ceremony,
Or our wedding even,
We were ready to call off the whole thing.

Until both of us sat,
Face to face,
At a Starbucks,
And re-evaluated everything.

On chits of paper,
We answered in writing,
Questions we were posing to each other.
If the answers matched,
We were meant to be.
If not, we would go our separate ways.

Thank that day.
We are still together.

Our love story is very 'filmy'.
Because we love being in love.
And bringing others together,

By inspiring them.

Being with Pratiik has taught me,
To win over any situation,
Handle it with love.

Loving Others

Being married to Pratiik is a commitment,
That I don't take lightly.

What's important to him is important to me.

In our lives,
Family and friends play an important role.

Loving your husband's family,
Receiving their love,
Keeping in touch,
These were not things that came naturally to me.
But I learned to appreciate these little things,
Over time.

Today, they are as much his family,
As they are mine.

Being married to me,
Is definitely not something Pratiik takes lightly
either.

He shows up,
In more ways than one.
He is a caregiver,

When I am low.
He is a cheer-me-up,
When I'm sad.
He is a contributor,
To most of my efforts.
He is a husband,
That redefines what it means,
To be one.

He considers my family his own.
Whether it's entertaining my nephew,
Or arranging coffee dates with my sister-in-law,
Or having a boys' night,
With the men in my family.
Or chilling endlessly with my parents,
When I am sleeping or lazy.
He mixes with everyone lovingly.

Ours is definitely a two way street,
And a two way marriage.

Being with Pratiik has taught me,
I have more love to give,
Than I give myself credit for.

What is Love?

So then there is the looming question.
What is love?

Is it what I felt when I was a child?
Is it what I felt when I was a teenager?
Is it what I felt in my mid-twenties?
Is it what I feel now, every day?
Is it what I felt for all those bygones?
Is it what I feel for everyone in my life?

It's simple and complicated.
No real answer, yet very real.

I think love is…

My husband and I,
Sharing little details of our days,
With so much importance.

My sister and I,
Talking in fake Chinese,
To entertain each other.

My mom and I,
Going around town,
When dad's not around.

My dad calling me,
Just to check
if I'm doing okay.

My brother-in-law,
Always remembering,
And amusing me with
Things I did way back when.

My mother-in-law,
Sharing reels on Instagram,
That will help me.

My father-in-law,
Calling to chat,
When he's low.

My brother-in-law,
And my co-sister,
Picking up cute gifts for me,
Whenever they travel.

My girlfriends,
Always entertaining me,
And talking to me for hours,
Irrespective of time zones.

Love truly is…
In the littlest things
That make our lives
LARGE.

Lessons of Love

Folks, these are the lessons I learnt,
Not setting out to love,
Accidentally falling head first,
In the deep end.

What not loving has taught me,
Is that love exists in all forms.

Love exists,
Even on the days
you have nothing to look forward to.
Even when you're
having a fight with someone.
Even when you're
filled to the brim and
can't take much more.

Love does make the world go round.
At least it does mine.
Even when I didn't set out to love.

9 789357 741880